GENOCIDE IN MODERN TIMES™

THE HOLOCAUST: JEWS, GERMANY, AND THE NATIONAL SOCIALISTS

James Norton

ROSEN
PUBLISHING®

New York

To those who fight against genocide, whoever and wherever they may be

Published in 2009 by The Rosen Publishing Group, Inc.
29 East 21st Street, New York, NY 10010

First Edition

Library of Congress Cataloging-in-Publication Data

Norton, James.
The Holocaust: Jews, Germany, and the National Socialists / James Norton.— 1st ed.
    p. cm.—(Genocide in modern times)
Includes bibliographical references and index.
ISBN-13: 978-1-4042-1821-5 (library binding)
1. Holocaust, Jewish (1939–1945)—Juvenile literature. 2. Jews—Persecutions—Germany—Juvenile literature. 3. World War, 1939–1945—Concentration camps—Juvenile literature. 4. Holocaust, Jewish (1939–1945)—Influence—Juvenile literature. I. Title.
D804.34.N67 2008
940.53'18—dc22

2007051813

Manufactured in the United States of America

On the cover: Foreground: A Russian politician lays a wreath at a Moscow monument to victims of the Holocaust. Background: Weak and emaciated victims of the Buchenwald concentration camp walk toward an infirmary following the Allied liberation of the camp.

CONTENTS

Introduction   4

1

The Rise of Hitler   8

2

The Jewish "Enemy"   16

3

The Death Camps   29

4

The Holocaust Today   44

Timeline   50

Glossary   53

For More Information   57

For Further Reading   60

Bibliography   61

Index   62

INTRODUCTION

Joseph Stalin, who was head of the Soviet Union during World War II and was responsible for the deaths of millions of people living within Soviet borders, said, "One death is a tragedy. A million deaths is just a statistic." He shrewdly realized that once the death toll rose to such incomprehensible numbers, people became deadened to genocide, or the mass murder of a specific ethnic, religious, racial, or political group of people. When talking about the Holocaust—the mass killing of Jews in Europe during World War II, which was orchestrated by another maniacal tyrant, Germany's Adolf Hitler—the number "six million" is often mentioned. It is thought by historians that somewhere between five and six million Jews were killed during the Holocaust, a number equivalent to three-quarters of the people currently living in New York City.

But numbers can't tell the entire story of the Holocaust. "Millions" of nameless,

A group of male survivors of the Buchenwald concentration camp grip a barbed-wire fence shortly after the camp's liberation by American forces in April 1945.

faceless victims isn't the same as a little girl named Anne Frank hiding in an attic in Amsterdam, praying that her family won't be found and sent to a death camp. It isn't the same as a ditch in the Ukraine filled with bodies—the village butcher, a musician, a shoemaker, a candle merchant, a student—all dead, all shot by German soldiers. It isn't the same as a trainload of freight cars packed full of shivering, half-naked people trying desperately to keep warm as they travel hundreds of miles from home to an unknown destination.

The very scope of the Holocaust (or *Shoah*, as it is called in Hebrew, the ancient language of the Jewish people) is such that it is hard to comprehend and come to terms with. But it is vital that Holocaust history is understood in order to remember and honor those who died and to prevent similar tragedies from happening again.

The Holocaust was a perversely well-organized mass-killing operation. It involved complicated train and truck routes, precisely organized military units, roll calls and census rosters, and an entire army of overseers, guards, executioners, and disposers of corpses. All this was undertaken during World War II, when Nazi Germany desperately needed its soldiers to wage war against its enemies, the Soviet Union, Great Britain, and the United States. But such was the Nazi hatred for Jews that it nevertheless devoted precious manpower to the creation, operation, and maintenance of concentration camps in which Jews, as well as Catholics, Gypsies, homosexuals, and other groups deemed "inferior," were imprisoned and murdered. Indeed, Germany's most important front in the war was not the western front, where U.S. and British forces massed, or the eastern front, where the mighty Soviet army loomed. Instead, Germany focused its a vital share of its energy and manpower within its territory, exterminating innocent and defenseless Jewish people, perceived by the Nazis to be Germany's longtime enemy and grave threat.

Before the rise of Hitler and his Nazi Party, Jews owned property, intermarried with Germans, served as faculty members at top universities, held political office, served with honor in the German military, and felt that they had successfully integrated into German society. Many regarded themselves as Germans first, Jews second. All this would come to end under Hitler's brutal rule.

Over the course of the Holocaust—beginning in the 1930s and ending with the end of World War II in 1945—somewhere between five and six million Jewish people would be killed (mostly in Germany and eastern Europe) by the Nazis and their allies. An entire cross section of German society participated in their imprisonment and killing, from churches that turned over birth records proving Jewish heritage, to postal workers who carried deportation orders, to companies that used Jews as slave labor or test subjects for experimental drugs. At the same time, ordinary people—in places like Poland, the Netherlands, France, and even in Germany—stood up to the killing machine, risking their own lives to save others.

Even today, there are arguments about how the Holocaust came to be and why it wasn't stopped. One thing remains clear: the rise to power of Adolf Hitler and his National Socialist (or Nazi) Party in Germany was the first domino in the chain that led to the most deliberate mass murder in the history of humankind.

1

The Rise of Hitler

Adolf Hitler was born in 1889 in Austria. Although not originally a German citizen, he would fight in the German army during World War I, which began in 1914. Germany's defeat in World War I was seen by many Germans—including Hitler—as a result of betrayal by weak political leaders and other enemies of the state. Because they stood out from the population at large, German Jews were popular targets for blame. They were accused by Hitler (and others) of undermining the war effort and working in safe jobs far from the front lines.

There is no historical evidence for this accusation whatsoever. Jews served with bravery in the German military, undertaking dangerous frontline jobs in large numbers, and often receiving medals for their efforts. Many died or were wounded in action. But because they had a different ethnic and religious identity from that of most Germans, they became a convenient scapegoat. In later years, during the Nazi regime, even Jews who had been decorated German officers would find that their patriotism was no shield. The only thing that mattered to the Nazis was that a person was Jewish, and that identification often served as a death certificate. Indeed, the Nazi government was willing to damage its own economic and cultural interests in order to pursue its campaign against the Jews.

German Jews—like the two depicted in the studio portrait to the right—served with honor and distinction in the country's armed forces during World War I.

THE GERMAN WORKERS' PARTY AND THE RISE OF NAZISM

After World War I came to an end in November 1918, Hitler became involved in German politics, joining a small right-wing organization called the German Workers' Party. Its members were angry about the Treaty of Versailles, which ended World War I. The treaty required Germany to pay money to the victorious Allied powers (including France and Britain), took various territories from Germany, and imposed limits on the German armed forces. All of this was seen as an outrage to German honor. A group of Germans called the November Criminals was blamed for stabbing the army in the back. A combination of Communists, Jews, and weak politicians were all blamed for the surrender, which was in fact a result of the inferiority of Germany's military and economy to those of the Allied Powers that opposed them.

By July 1921, Hitler had seized control of the German Workers' Party, now called the National Socialist—or Nazi—Party. Hitler was an impressive speaker. Emotional, sarcastic, passionate, and filled with rage, he could hold a room full of people at attention for hours at a

Before attaining power as the dictator of Germany, Adolf Hitler (shown here in 1925) was a powerful and popular public speaker. Among his favorite targets were Jews, Communists, and anyone seen as having contributed to Germany's defeat in World War I.

time. Although he was seen as an unimportant figure by the country's major right-wing politicians, they often harnessed his passion and dedicated followers to suit their purposes. The Nazis could stir up street violence and push for radical right-wing solutions that more mainstream politicians could not, or would not, advocate. And they represented a small but increasingly vocal and influential number of voters on election day.

At first, Hitler and the Nazis were not interested in winning power peacefully or through a legitimate electoral process. There were too many obstacles to clear and too many more powerful and popular parties to beat. The seizure of Italy's government in 1922 by Fascist leader Benito Mussolini inspired Hitler and his followers to attempt a similar grab at

Hitler and his allies faced trial for their attempted putsch (takeover of government) in 1923. The man to the left of Hitler is General Erich Ludendorff, a popular right-wing military figure whose involvement with Hitler's cause gave the future dictator prestige and credibility.

power in Germany. On November 8, 1923, the Nazi Party attempted to take over the major German state of Bavaria. But the attempt was a disaster. Sixteen Nazis were killed, the revolt was crushed by the military, and Hitler and other leading party leaders were put on trial.

MEIN KAMPF

Hitler turned his trial into a platform for his poisonous political philosophy. A sympathetic judge let him speak for hours about his plans for Germany. Although he was sentenced to five years in a comfortable prison, the trial turned him into a national celebrity. He was seen as a man of action and one of the only people brave enough to fight for

Adolf Hitler's autobiography, *Mein Kampf*, is seen here as a display at the Yad Vashem Holocaust Memorial in Jerusalem, Israel. The book was an early warning of his destructive intentions.

Germany's honor and against the unpopular Treaty of Versailles. In prison, he visited with fellow jailed Nazis, read mail from like-minded admirers, and entertained guests. Meanwhile, he put his ideas into print, working on his autobiography. Entitled *Mein Kampf* ("My Struggle"), it told the story of Hitler's "heroic" fight against the enemies of Germany. In it, many future actions—including the persecution of Jews and his attempted conquest of Europe—were clearly discussed.

One of *Mein Kampf*'s central themes was how the weak or otherwise "unfit" should be sacrificed to benefit the good of the majority. Hitler wrote: "It is a half-measure to let incurably sick people steadily contaminate the remaining healthy ones. This is in keeping with the humanitarianism which, to avoid hurting one individual, lets a hundred others perish. The demand that defective people be prevented from propagating equally defective offspring is a demand of the clearest reason and, if systematically executed, represents the most humane act of mankind."

This sort of argument was the bedrock of Nazi theory, and *Mein Kampf* was full of it: essentially, that the weak should be sterilized or even eliminated (although Hitler was careful to avoid explicitly calling for murder) in order that others may live and prosper. His willingness to label human beings as "defective" or un-German set the stage for the killings to come later on. And those who read between the lines of the book could find plenty of evidence that Hitler would take action to jail and even kill anyone who was seen as an enemy of Germany, including racial "enemies" such as the Jews.

Published in 1925 and 1926, *Mein Kampf* sold about 240,000 copies between 1925 and 1934. Eventually, after the Nazi takeover of the country, about ten million copies would be sold or handed out for free. *Mein Kampf* and Hitler's triumphant trial turned him into the undisputed leader of the Nazis. As a party, the Nazis moved from the freedom of having internal debates and elected leadership to a totalitarian system wherein Hitler's word was always final. Later, when the Nazis would eventually gain power in Germany, a similar shift—from democracy to dictatorship—would take place.

Reinhard Heydrich (1904–1942)

Reinhard Heydrich was the head of security under Hitler's government. He led the Reich Main Security Office, which included the notorious secret police, the Gestapo. He was responsible for building the Gestapo into a terrifying weapon of state power. So cruel were his methods that even his fellow Nazis viewed him as a butcher.

Heydrich's most notorious contribution to the Holocaust was the chairing of the 1942 Wannsee Conference. At this gathering, plans were finalized for the destruction of all of Europe's Jews. Heydrich was shot by British-trained Czechoslovak soldiers in Prague on May 27, 1942, in an assassination attempt. He died a week later.

HITLER INCITES HATRED AND SEIZES POWER

The Great Depression—a period of worldwide economic collapse that resulted in the impoverishment and ruin of millions of people—provided Hitler and the Nazis with a golden opportunity to seize power. Many Germans were unemployed. They were angry, desperate, and hungry. They wanted enemies to blame for their country's weakness and the collapse of the economy, and Hitler offered them someone to blame and hate. Aggressive campaigning built up the Nazi Party's popularity even as the democratically elected government, the Weimar Republic, floundered in search of solutions. Hitler was a master of propaganda, which is the use of words, music, images, and other forms of communication to hammer home political messages. By playing on prejudice, fear, national pride, and hatred, he built up the Nazi Party into a national organization.

Hitler and the Nazis now ran energetically for political office, seeking to take power by legal means. Although the Nazis often fought in the streets with their political opponents (mostly with the Communists), they

Adolf Hitler shakes hands with a traditionally dressed peasant girl in Buckeburg, Germany, in 1937. Though he held radical views on race and politics, Hitler liked to associate himself with traditional, conservative German images.

also fought at the ballot box. In 1932, Hitler campaigned by airplane—a first in Germany—and came in second in a national election. A once-marginal politician who stirred his audiences with a patriotism based upon prejudice and hatred had come to the forefront of the country with votes, not guns.

After another year of political wrangling, Hitler finally managed to get himself appointed chancellor of Germany on January 30, 1933. A month later, the Reichstag building—the "Congress" of Germany where elected representatives met to debate and vote on legislation—was set on fire, an act blamed on a Communist. This gave Hitler's new government the chance it was looking for to crack down on political opponents. The German Communist Party, the main rival to the Nazis, was banned. New elections undertaken in an atmosphere of fear gave the Nazi Party an even stronger hold on the government. Nazi laws eliminated or restricted civil liberties, such as a right to a fair trial and protection against being jailed without just cause.

Because Germans were scared of Communist terrorism (like the Reichstag fire) and wanted a strong leader to ensure the rebuilding of the armed forces greatly weakened by the Versailles Treaty, there was little resistance to the Nazi takeover. By August 1933, with the death of the country's president (whose powers were then given to Hitler) and the passage of legislation making Hitler's power unquestionable, the Nazis had taken absolute control of Germany. The voters and other political parties, including the main Catholic party, had willingly given power to the Nazi Party in a time of trouble, and the Nazi Party had made that gift permanent. There would be no more challenges from opponents seeking to use elections to dispute Nazi ideas.

2

The Jewish "Enemy"

Soon after the Nazi Party's rise to power in 1933, Jews began leaving the country. Some 37,000 German Jews, mostly with strong international connections and/or wealth, left for other parts of the world. Anti-Semitic Nazi propaganda had convinced many non-Jewish Germans that Jews were not "real" Germans. In fact, they were believed to be parasites, living off of other people's work and contributing nothing. The Nazi Party contrasted Jews unfavorably to ethnic Germans. "Real" Germans, party propaganda said, were strong, creative, loyal, healthy, and handsome. Jews, by contrast, represented disease, greed, immorality, and a weakening of the national character.

This propaganda ignored the fact that Jews were in fact great contributors to German economic, intellectual, creative, and artistic vitality. Jews were professors, bankers, professional musicians, artists, craftspeople, factory workers, merchants, and scientists. Some of the most economically and culturally important people in the country were Jewish. This changed with the rise of the Nazis, however. Jews were encouraged—sometimes with threats and violence—to leave the country. Jewish businesses were bought out by non-Jewish Germans, often because of threats and menacing by the police.

Public notices like this one served to alert Germans to the anti-Jewish boycott of April 1, 1933. This poster was drafted by the Central Committee for the Defense Against Jewish Atrocities.

MARGINALIZING JEWISH GERMANS

On April 1, 1933, Hitler declared a national boycott of businesses that were owned by Jews. The Nazi leadership suggested that Jews were "the guilty ones" responsible for the country's economic problems, who "live in our midst and day after day misuse the right to hospitality, which the German Volk [people] has granted them." The effects of the boycott were felt all across the country. Jews who had lived for generations in Germany were made to feel as though they were no longer really Germans but were instead foreigners who had worn out their welcome.

In *Holocaust: A History,* authors Deborah Dwork and Robert Jan van Pelt, tell the story of a Jewish family living in a small southern German town:

> In the morning before classes, we would all congregate in the Turnplatz [gym field] where we played. I remember the boys were on one side and the girls on the other side, and we were playing ball. We were standing there, these four girls, four of us, and no one ever threw the ball to us. That's when we knew. That was it. That day of the boycott, April 1, 1933, that was really the watershed. After that, it was as if we weren't there.

Joseph Goebbels (1897–1945)

Adolf Hitler's right-hand man and minister for propaganda, Dr. Paul Joseph Goebbels, is among those most responsible for the poisonous atmosphere that led to the marginalization, demonization, imprisonment, and death of six million of Europe's Jews. As editor of the Berlin Nazi newspaper *Der Angriff* ("The Attack") in the 1920s, Goebbels fought tirelessly to advance the Nazi cause, savagely attacking Jews and left-wing opponents while doing so. After the Nazis came to power in 1933, Goebbels organized a mass burning of books by Jewish and other "subversive" authors. He also drove Jews out of their jobs in journalism, film, publishing, music, and literature.

The first major event in Goebbels's long record of anti-Semitism was his organizing of the Kristallnacht attacks of 1938. His attitude only hardened as the years went by. Writing in his diary in 1942, Goebbels was pitiless toward the Jews: "In general, it can probably be established that 60 percent of them must be liquidated, while only 40 percent can be put to work . . . A judgment is being carried out on the Jews which is barbaric, but fully deserved." At the war's end, as Allied forces seized Berlin, Goebbels and his wife, Magda, killed their six children before killing themselves.

Shown in a 1933 photo, Joseph Goebbels is sitting during a trip abroad to attend the League of Nations (the precursor to the modern United Nations).

A woman reads a sign in a shop window warning Germans to only buy at German shops. The 1933 anti-Jewish boycott is seen by many as the turning point toward Nazi genocide.

Deutsche, verteidigt euch gegen die jüdische Greuelpropaganda, kauft nur bei Deutschen!

Germans defend yourselves against jewish atrocity propaganda

buy only at German shops!

Within weeks of the boycott, Jewish people were banned by law from working in the civil service (low-ranking government positions) and the legal profession. This was part of an emerging pattern: by removing Jews from positions of influence, from which they could speak out, it made them far less visible and far less able to object to the treatment they were receiving. Soon, Jewish students were banned from public schools, and Jewish doctors were thrown out of national hospitals. The first step to destroying a people is to make them invisible, and this is a task that the Nazis undertook nearly as soon as they were elected.

At the same time that the Jews were being removed from public life and stripped of their rights, other segments of the German population were suffering under Nazi control. Forced sterilizations of the mentally handicapped, blind, deaf, mentally ill, and habitual criminals resulted in some four hundred thousand people being stripped of their ability to have children. All of this was part of the Nazi plan for a "master race." Germany, said Hitler, was to be the land of the "pure" and "superior" Aryans—northern Europeans such as Germans and Scandinavians.

This German propaganda slide from 1934 features images of two physically disabled children. The original caption on the slide read "deformed." Emphasizing the alien nature of entire groups of people was one way that the Nazis set the stage for mass murder.

Slavic people (like Russians and many eastern Europeans), Gypsies (Roma), Jews, those of African descent, and the mentally or physically handicapped were deemed to be "impure" and "inferior," and millions of them would be exterminated as a result.

THE ROLE OF ORDINARY GERMANS

Why did Germans go along with this deranged and nonsensical Nazi plan to create a false sense of racial purity? Hitler and his government were aggressive in working to rebuild the country's armed forces and reassert its power on the world stage. During a period of great confusion and ambivalence, Nazis offered strong, absolute, black-and-white answers. And anti-Semitism had been a force in Germany, and throughout all of Europe, for centuries. Although the Nazi brand of anti-Semitism was based on crackpot theories presented as though they were carefully researched, it tapped into old tribal fears about the neighbor who doesn't go to church and doesn't share all the same traditions as the German Catholic or Protestant family next door.

Many ordinary Germans were scared by the Nazis, who were happy to imprison those who spoke out. And many Germans saw an advantage to stripping the Jews of their power and property. Non-Jews stood to take

Oskar Schindler (1908–1974)

Not all Germans aided the Nazi's Holocaust efforts or stood by silently and did nothing while the killing continued. Some worked against it. Oskar Schindler, an ammunition and enamelware manufacturer in Germany, is credited with saving 1,200 Jews by having them work in his factories. Schindler used his Nazi Party membership, charm, persuasion, bribes, and trickery to protect his Jewish workers and their families and to keep himself out of jail.

In 1993, Schindler's story reached much of the world by way of Steven Spielberg's Holocaust movie *Schindler's List*. Schindler's motives were unclear. But through the course of the war and the Holocaust, he was transformed from a self-interested businessman into the savior of more than a thousand lives. An interview with Schindler may reveal some of what motivated him to act: "I knew the people who worked for me . . . When you know people, you have to behave toward them like human beings" (as quoted in an article by the *Independent*).

their jobs, their homes, and their businesses. A combination of fear and greed undermined any help and protection these Germans might have offered to their Jewish neighbors. The Jews were left exposed and defenseless to Nazi harassment and violence.

INCREASING OPPRESSION

In the years following the Nazi regime's rise to power, the persecution of Jews got worse. The government used something called the salami technique—discrimination enacted one thin slice at a time. By mid-1935, signs on shop windows declaring "Jews and dogs not welcome" and "No Jews served" became commonplace. Within a couple of years, what was once a thriving mainstream part of the German population had been removed from public life. Jews were thrown out of hospitals, courtrooms, universities, the armed forces, and almost any place that could be used as a platform for self-defense or pride.

Paradoxically, new Jewish cultural and religious associations sprung up in this hostile environment, and the identity of the community was actually strengthened by this persecution. But these new associations couldn't protect Jews from the ferocity of an angry German government and people. More and more violent actions were taken against Jews. Germans wrecked Jewish shops, beat Jewish people, and took the law into their own hands. Police rarely, if ever, intervened to protect Jews from their former countrymen.

In 1936, Berlin hosted the summer Olympic Games, which led to a temporary die-down in anti-Jewish hostility as the world's eyes were

The yellow star on the overcoat of this middle-class German Jew (photographed in 1935) made him a target for harassment and abuse. Jews who failed to wear their stars were subject to even harsher punishment if discovered.

Conditions for Jews and other unpopular minorities improved briefly during the 1936 Berlin Olympics but quickly worsened after the games ended and attention from the outside world shifted elsewhere.

turned to Germany. But things worsened again in 1937. The Nuremberg Rally, a massive party meeting in the German town of the same name, confirmed Hitler's plans to racially "unite" the country by removing the Jewish population. Under the slogan *Ein Reich, Ein Volk, Ein Fuhrer* ("One Empire, One People, One Leader"), Hitler asserted German racial power and vowed to bring all Germanic peoples together into one super-country. This was followed in 1938 by the unification of Austria and Germany.

The German empire was growing. And as it did, more and more Jews became victims of its racism. In Austria, soon after German troops marched in, Jews were forced to clean the pavement on their hands and knees, using toothbrushes and a cleaning solution made with acid. Many were sent to concentration camps, which were at this point mostly holding pens for political prisoners and "undesirables," such as the Jews. Although conditions were bad, the camps had not yet become places of mass death.

Mass rallies, such as this one in Nuremberg in 1936, were a key way for the Nazi Party to frighten its enemies and impress its supporters. With their incredible displays of military power, rallies were powerful propaganda.

In November 1938, Germans rioted against Jews in what became known as Kristallnacht. A worker *(left)* cleans up glass from a broken shop window following the riot in Berlin.

KRISTALLNACHT

A key turning point came on November 7, 1938. A young Jewish man named Herschel Grynszpan, angered over the expulsion of his parents from Germany, shot a German diplomat named Ernst vom Rath, who was stationed in Paris, France. The shooting was immediately reported by Nazi newspapers and turned into an excuse for a string of attacks on nearly ten thousand Jewish businesses and more than a thousand places of worship. The violence, which stretched across Germany, became known as Kristallnacht, the "Night of Broken Glass." Shop windows were shattered, homes were trashed by Germans wielding axes and clubs, Jews were imprisoned and beaten to death, Jewish cemeteries were vandalized, and more than 1,500 synagogues (Jewish temples) were burned.

Many historians say that Kristallnacht was the true beginning of the Holocaust, the moment in which the German government's campaign against Jews moved from stripping them of their legal rights and driving them out of the country toward the destruction of property and extermination of people. The pretense that the German government was taking rights away from Jews in order to protect or shelter them had

Anne Frank (1929–1945)

Annelies Marie "Anne" Frank was born in Frankfurt, Germany, in 1929. Born into a Reform Jewish family, her father was a decorated German officer from World War I—a fact that would do nothing to

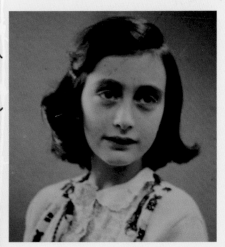

help the family during the Holocaust. Anne fled Germany with her family in early 1934 after the Nazi Party won local elections.

The Franks ended up in the Netherlands, a temporary safe haven for Jews. But the Nazis invaded and occupied the Netherlands in 1940. By July 1942, the family was living in a hiding place above her father's workplace. An informant's tip led to the family's arrest in 1944, and Anne and her sister were shipped off to Bergen-Belsen concentration camp. Both would die there in 1945.

This portrait of Anne Frank, taken in May 1939, is from her own photo album.

Her father, however, survived the ordeal and returned to Amsterdam. Having been informed of his daughters' deaths and recovering Anne's diary of their time in hiding, he fulfilled Anne's wish to become an author. In 1947, Anne Frank's diary was published.

Anne's observations about the ongoing Holocaust—the constant fear of discovery and arrest, the struggle to eat, the cruelty of ordinary people—were often dark. But she kept a sense of optimism, even amid the darkest of circumstances: "I don't think of all the misery, but of the beauty that still remains . . . My advice is: 'Go outside, to the fields, enjoy nature and the sunshine, go out and try to recapture happiness in yourself and in God. Think of all the beauty that's still left in and around you and be happy!'"

now fallen completely apart, and naked hatred had become the order of the day. Nazi police and special troops known as the SS (the "protective squadron" that was personally answerable to Hitler) helped organize Kristallnacht, and SS members would be the key leaders of later efforts to contain and destroy Jews throughout Nazi-occupied Europe.

Increasingly after Kristallnacht, Jews were removed from their homes, stripped of their belongings, and shipped off to ghettos. Ghettos were special concentrations of city blocks walled off and restricted to Jews only. In cities such as Warsaw, Jews slept nine people to a room, a recipe for disease and misery. The concentration of Jews into ghettos helped non-Jews forget about their existence and made later steps— such as shipping them off in freight cars to concentration camps—much easier to accomplish.

3

The Death Camps

The places where millions of Jews were imprisoned and then killed are generally known as concentration camps. Camps built and used solely for killing prisoners were known more specifically as extermination or death camps. Built in the early days of the Nazi government, concentration camps were originally designed to hold political prisoners and other "undesirables" such as Roma, or Gypsies. Jews were sometimes rounded up and placed in these camps.

While conditions were often terrible, they weren't originally meant to hold prisoners for long periods of time, nor were they designed to be places where prisoners would be systematically killed. With the advent of the war, however, conditions in the camps began to change radically. Camps took on a role in the German economy, providing slave labor designed to help the war effort. Major German corporations willingly used this slave labor. It was cheaper than paying regular workers (who were in short supply following the outbreak of World War II) and was seen as patriotic.

Additionally, the camps began to fill with prisoners of war (mostly Soviet) who were treated extremely poorly. An estimated three million Soviet prisoners would die in camps before the end

A single Nazi German paratrooper guards a group of captured Soviet troops in 1942, forcing them to march with their hands on their heads. Millions of Soviet troops eventually died in German prisoner-of-war camps.

of war. Some estimates, accounting for prisoners shot on the spot by German troops, suggest that as many as five million Soviet prisoners were killed by the Nazis throughout the course of the war. As the fight against the Allies grew harder, the quest for the "Final Solution" became more desperate.

THE "FINAL SOLUTION"

The true turning point came in 1942, in a Berlin meeting known as the Wannsee Conference. This meeting, attended by high-level Nazi members of government, finally settled an argument that had been taking place among Hitler's advisers. Some of Hitler's ministers thought that Jews were best used as slave labor and a bargaining chip in case of an Allied victory. But a more influential group thought that the time had come to exterminate the Jews once and for all. The German governor of occupied Poland, Hans Frank, speaking a month before the conference, said, "We must destroy the Jews wherever we find them and wherever it is possible to do so" (according to public Nuremburg Trial documents).

Tragically, Frank's remarks echoed the tone of the Wannsee meeting, which took place on January 20, 1942. Minutes of the meeting show a

Nazi official Hans Frank parades in an open car in Graz, Austria, on January 1, 1938. He would later become the Nazi administrator of occupied Poland and would play a key role in the Holocaust.

general agreement that the eleven to twelve million Jews throughout Europe (including portions not yet and never to be conquered by Germany) should be deported to camps to work in labor gangs, with the hope of working some—if not most—of them to death. The approval of a mass movement of Jews and the general agreement that death was an acceptable and even desirable end for them set the stage for the killing that was to come. Once it was agreed at the highest levels of Hitler's government that Jewish communities should be uprooted and put under the direct control of the SS, the crowding, disease, and eventual extermination of Jewish prisoners that followed was all but inevitable.

Heinrich Himmler (1900–1945)

Heinrich Himmler controlled the SS—Nazi Germany's elite armed police—and, to some degree, all of Germany's police and security forces during the war. Himmler was the founder and commander of the concentration camps and the Einsatzgruppen mobile death squads. He professed a belief in the superiority of the Aryan race and believed that selective breeding could engineer the German populace to be entirely "Nordic" in appearance within several decades.

On October 4, 1943, Himmler spoke explicitly about the ongoing killing of the Jewish people during an SS meeting in Poznan, Poland: "I also want to mention a very difficult subject before you here, completely openly. It should be discussed amongst us, and yet, nevertheless, we will never speak about it in public. I am talking about the Jewish evacuation: the extermination of the Jewish people" (according to a transcription of tape retrieved from the Nuremberg Trials). In 1945, he committed suicide after being captured by the British army.

THE NAZI KILLING MACHINE

Before the Wannsee Conference had even happened, the Germans had been using poison gas vans and roving firing squads to kill Jews in occupied Russia and Poland. Nazi leaders such as Heinrich Himmler, Adolf Eichmann, and Reinhard Heydrich had approved of a campaign to kill Jews by whatever means necessary. This sometimes meant rounding up families of Jews, throwing them into locked air-tight vans, and then turning on a flow of poisoned gas. Sometimes the gas failed, leaving the people inside to die a slow death of suffocation.

Eventually, the gas vans fell out of use. Mobile firing squads called Einsatzgruppen killed an estimated 1.3 million Jews (according to historian Raul Hilberg) in countries such as Lithuania, Russia, Ukraine, and Poland. SS men and volunteers would shoot prisoners in groups and dump the bodies into long trench-like mass graves. Entire Jewish communities would be massacred like this, with women and children dying alongside men.

Deborah Dwork and Robert Jan van Pelt's book *Holocaust* lays out a bird's-eye view of Treblinka,

After the war, investigators found evidence of genocide, like this map entitled "Jewish Executions Carried Out by Einsatzgruppe A." Numbers near coffins are estimates of the Jews killed in particular territories.

one of the most deadly of the extermination camps, in early 1943. About three-quarters of a million people were eventually killed at Treblinka, which was in peak operation from July 1942 through October 1943. Located northeast of Warsaw, Poland, it was centrally positioned to be a destination for Europe's Jews. The camp was surrounded by antitank defenses. Like all Nazi concentration camps, it was militarized so as to prevent escape from within or rescue from outside. A railway spur connected the camp to the main line of the railroad so that Jews and others could be brought into the camp in large numbers.

After arriving at the camp, valuables were taken from prisoners. Any who seemed as though they might resist were brought into a sham "hospital" and shot. Most of the new arrivals were brought to an undressing barracks, after which they were directed straight to the gas chambers. Carbon monoxide was then used to kill large groups of people at once. By the end of the camp's existence, it featured thirteen gas chambers. After victims were killed with gas, their gold teeth were extracted, and their bodies were burned on "roasts." The ashes were buried in mass graves. The cremation and burial portions of the camp were screened from the rest of the operation by earthen walls so as to not panic the prisoners. In addition to Treblinka, a number of other camps, including Chelmno, Belzec, and Sobibor, were solely used for killing. Auschwitz (with its satellite death camp of Birkenau) and Majdanek were built for other reasons, but they were eventually also transformed into execution sites.

The trauma suffered by families arriving at these camps cannot be overstated. Many knew or strongly suspected that death awaited them. Upon arriving at camps, most families were separated by guards. Helen Lebowitz Goldkind, a survivor of the Auschwitz camp who told her story on the U.S. Holocaust Memorial Museum's Web site, describes what it was like to arrive at the camp:

Then you see these mothers coming down with little kids, and they're . . . and they're trying to pull these kids out of their

Children stand behind a barbed-wire fence at Auschwitz, in modern-day Poland. German death camps spared no one: the young, the old, the healthy, and the sick all died within their walls.

mother's hands. And you know, when you try to separate a family, it's very difficult. It's very difficult. People put up fights. It . . . it, there was so much screams. So, there was a truck. I remember that truck. So, the parents, the . . . the mothers that wouldn't give up these children, and they, they were beaten up, and the kids got hurt, so they grabbed these kids, and they threw them on the truck, and they really didn't look how they were throwing them on the truck. So, at that time, we saw that something horrible is happening—the way these people were behaving to little children, to little babies. And, of course, on that truck there were people, you know, very sick people going, you know, they were throwing sick people there, and . . . and . . . and these children that gave them a tough time. They were just thrown on the trucks. And there were so many mothers that were running after the trucks, and, of course, they beat them, and they pushed them back.

While gassing and cremation were the most direct ways that extermination camps were used to kill prisoners, many were killed in the camps by overcrowding, starvation, overwork, and disease. The very act of uprooting people from their homes and forcing them into inhumane conditions in camp was life-threatening, and many of the first victims were children and the elderly.

JEWISH RESISTANCE

Although overwhelmed by the strength of the armed guards who patrolled the camps, Jews made many efforts to resist, staging uprisings in the death camps whenever possible. On August 2, 1943, prisoners at Treblinka seized weapons from the camp armory. Hundreds of prisoners stormed the main gate in an attempt to escape. Three hundred got out, but two-thirds of those who did were tracked down and killed by German SS and police units, as well as units from the German military.

Mordechaj Anielewicz (1919–1943)

A Polish Jew born to a poor family near Warsaw, Mordechaj Anielewicz would grow up to become a leader in the fight against the Nazi occupation of Poland. As a young twenty-something, he became chief commander of the Jewish Fighting Organization in the Warsaw ghetto.

In January 1943, Anielewicz was instrumental in leading the fighting that would prevent a shipment of Jews from being deported from the ghetto into the concentration camps, where the Jewish prisoners would have been killed. This first ghetto uprising was followed by another fight that was finally put down by German forces in May of the same year. Anielewicz and his girlfriend, Mira Fuchrer, were both killed in the street battle, along with many of their comrades. Anielewicz has been remembered as one of the heroes of the Holocaust for fighting a doomed fight—against extremely long odds—to keep Jews from being slaughtered by the Germans.

At Birkenau (the death camp of Auschwitz) on October 7, 1944, Jewish Sonderkommandos staged a revolt. (Sonderkommandos were inmates put to work in the gas chambers and crematoria.) They used axes, tools, rocks, and homemade grenades to take SS guards by surprise and destroy one of the crematoria. Although hundreds of prisoners escaped, all were soon recaptured. Many other armed resistance and escape attempts were made, although the vast majority failed. Starving, unarmed prisoners were usually no match for well-fed guards armed with machine guns.

It should be noted that in the rush to destroy Europe's Jews, many other groups of people were sacrificed to the Nazi death machine as well. Jehovah's Witnesses, Roman Catholic Poles, homosexuals, Roma, and many others were killed. And while many Jewish victims came from

Vidkun Quisling (1887–1945)

The occupied peoples of Europe took a number of different stances toward the Nazi occupiers. Some governments fled and fought the Nazis from exile. Some government officials resigned, to be replaced by Germans. And some ordinary citizens from occupied countries collaborated, helping the Germans to deport Jews and fight the war against the Allies.

Vidkun Quisling was a Norwegian Fascist politician who welcomed the 1940 Nazi invasion of his country and became Norway's minister president under German rule. During his term of service, he was responsible for recruiting his fellow citizens to serve in the Norwegian SS division, deporting Jews (to almost certain death in concentration camps) and executing Norwegian patriots. After the war, Quisling was executed for treason. To this day, calling someone a Quisling is the same thing as calling him or her a traitor.

Germany and occupied Poland, many other Jewish prisoners came from Nazi-occupied countries like France, Hungary, Norway, and the Netherlands.

LIBERATION

For many imprisoned in the concentration camps, there was disbelief that the Allies hadn't done more to stop their suffering. U.S. planes could have bombed the trains leading to the camps. Although some prisoners would have been killed, some might have escaped, and the means of transportation to the camps would have been shattered. But American priorities were centered on beating the German army, not stopping a genocide that many American leaders remained unconvinced was even taking place.

Furnaces like this one (a replica seen at the museum at Auschwitz, Poland) were used to destroy the bodies of camp victims. The original furnace destroyed the bodies of an estimated seventy thousand people between 1940 and 1943.

The end of World War II in May 1945 didn't immediately bring an end to the suffering of those in concentration camps. Tragically, many prisoners, starving and weakened by disease, died even after troops from the Soviet or American armies arrived to liberate their camps. The situation that greeted Soviet troops arriving at Auschwitz was heartbreaking. In *Hitler: Nemesis*, Ian Kershaw writes:

On January 26 [1945], an SS unit blew up the last of the crematoria in Birkenau. The next day, the SS guards retreated in heavy fighting as Soviet troops liberated the 7,000 exhausted, skeleton-like prisoners they found in the Auschwitz camp-complex. They also found 368,820 men's suits, 836,244 women's coats and dresses, 5,525 pairs of women's shoes, 13,964 carpets, large quantities of

The construction of the Buchenwald camp began July 15, 1937. Almost eight years later, on April 1, 1945, it was liberated by U.S. general George Patton's army. An estimated fifty-six thousand people died at the camp.

children's clothes, toothbrushes, false teeth, pots and pans, and a vast amount of human hair.

Many of the concentration camp prisoners who were healthy enough to walk when Allied forces began to close in found themselves forced into death marches through the snow by their fleeing Nazi captors. Many

Primo Levi (1919–1987)

A Jewish Italian chemist and survivor of Auschwitz, Primo Levi is one of the best-known and most respected contributors to the field of Holocaust literature. Levi's promising career in chemistry was cut short due to racial purity laws in Italy that prevented Italian companies from

employing highly educated Jews. In 1943, he joined anti-Fascist guerrillas but was quickly captured. He was then exiled to Auschwitz because of his Jewish ancestry. He arrived at the camp with 650 other Jews from the same "shipment." Eleven months later, when the camp was liberated by the Soviet army, he was one of only twenty to have survived the experience.

After the war, Levi became a respected chemist and wrote *If This Is a Man*, an account of his time in Auschwitz. A product of Levi bearing witness to what he had seen, it was a weapon in his fight against the growing phenomenon of Holocaust denial. In 2006, Levi's *The Periodic Table*, a collection of short stories each named for a different physical element, was recognized as the best science book ever by the Royal Institution of Great Britain.

dropped dead as they walked. Those too weak to move on were sometimes shot by their guards. In one march from Auschwitz alone, eight hundred prisoners were murdered by their guards, sometimes for stopping briefly, sometimes for no reason whatsoever.

Jewish survivors of the Buchenwald camp, shown here standing on the deck of the refugee immigration ship *Mataroa* on July, 15 1945, were among those who settled what would become the state of Israel.

ONGOING SUFFERING

An estimated one hundred thousand Jewish survivors of the camps found themselves swamped amid almost seven million other uprooted and homeless European people who were classified by the Allies as displaced persons (DPs). For months, the camp survivors and other DPs wandered throughout Europe, trying to make their way home. But for the Jews—known later as *Sh'erit ha-Pletah*, a Biblical term meaning "the Surviving Remnant"—"home" was not necessarily where it used to be. Anti-Semitism and the destruction of their old communities meant that emigration to countries such as Palestine (the land that would become the modern state of Israel, which was still under the control of the British) and the United States was the only real option left.

Organized in refugee camps in Austria, Germany, and Italy, the Jewish DPs quickly organized themselves, putting together their own governing associations and cultural, educational, and social groups. As months stretched into years, they began working with the world humanitarian community to push for the British to let more Jews into Palestine and for the American government to loosen the strict immigration laws keeping Jews from coming to the United States.

The Holocaust Today

Looking back at the Holocaust, it is sometimes hard to believe that such an unimaginably terrifying and horrific event took place. Indeed, Holocaust deniers have tried to use the very scope of the disaster to argue that it could not possibly have happened. But numerous writers and Holocaust victims such as Elie Wiesel, Primo Levi, and Anne Frank recorded personal memories of the genocide. Census records and Nazi documents confirm the vast numbers of people who disappeared into the Holocaust, as do mass graves, the vast Auschwitz concentration camp complex (now preserved as a museum), and a host of other pieces of physical evidence, such as the thousands of eyeglasses taken from prisoners before their trip to the gas chamber.

First and foremost, the evidence collected at the post-war international tribunal held in Nuremberg represents a record—mostly written by Nazis themselves—of the massive industrial effort that was required to mount a killing campaign of the scale and intensity of the Holocaust. By holding the Nuremberg Trials, the Allied powers didn't merely bring Nazi war criminals such as Polish governor Hans Frank to account. They also ensured that the memories of the millions of people killed in the genocide would live on. The world's verdict of guilty at Nuremburg and the

Nazi leader Hermann Goering (shown in the witness box at the Nuremberg Trials in this March 16, 1946, photo) was one of the highest-ranking Nazis tried for war crimes. He managed to escape being executed by committing suicide with cyanide on October 15, 1946.

punishments handed down would also serve as a warning to future generations about the patterns and consequences of the Holocaust.

NEVER AGAIN!: REMEMBERING THE HOLOCAUST

Around the world, Holocaust museums have been built to preserve the stories of victims and survivors and to pay testament to the courage of those who challenged the Nazi regime. Some of the most significant include the Yad Vashem Memorial in Israel, the U.S. Holocaust Memorial

Christoph Melli was fired from his job at a Swiss bank after denouncing the bank for destroying documents about its handling of accounts belonging to victims of Naziism. When he visited Israel in September 1997, he was given a hero's welcome. He is shown here visiting the Yad Vashem museum in Jerusalem.

Museum in Washington, D.C., and the Simon Wiesenthal Center in Los Angeles, California. All are dedicated, at least in part, to the philosophy of "Never Again"—never again should genocide stain the ground with the blood of the innocent, whatever their religion, race, or nation might be. All these museums put stories to names, helping to transform the anonymous "six million" into real people who lived, breathed, laughed, cried, worked, played, and died. The U.S. Holocaust Memorial Museum has launched a Web project known as BENAS (Behind Every Name a Story) that allows survivors to tell their stories in essays that are then

Hans Frank (1900–1946)

A leading Nazi Party member, Hans Frank rose from his position as Hitler's legal advisor to a ministerial role in the wartime German government. Frank served as governor-general for the occupied Polish territories. He was instrumental in forcing Polish Jews into the ghettos, from which they would later be shipped into the country's death camps. Hitler promised Frank, on the eve of the invasion of Russia, that Jews would be eliminated from his Polish territory.

After the war, at the Nuremburg Trials, Frank was found guilty of war crimes. Among his fellow prisoners, he was unique in accepting at least some share of guilt for what had happened under his command: "My conscience does not allow me simply to throw the responsibility simply on minor people . . . A thousand years will pass and still Germany's guilt will not have been erased" (according to public Nuremburg Trial documents). Frank was executed in 1946.

posted online. In addition, around the world, Jewish families and others observe Yom HaShoah, or Holocaust Remembrance Day. Inaugurated in 1959, Yom HaShoah is a national day of memorial in Israel.

Because of the detailed records kept by the Nazi regime and the dedication that Holocaust survivors have shown toward the mission of remembering the genocide, the Holocaust has become known throughout the world. It provides a stark warning about how ordinary people can make poor decisions and put extraordinarily bad politicians into positions of power. It also teaches of the dangerous power of language and imagery—how racist speech and images aren't merely emotionally hurtful but can also be physically destructive—as it sets the stage for far more violent crimes.

Elie Wiesel (b. 1928)

A French-Romanian Jewish Holocaust survivor, Elie Wiesel was awarded the Nobel Peace Prize in 1986 for his work as a writer, opponent of racism, and advocate of peace. His best-known work is *Night*, the extremely influential Holocaust memoir originally published in 1958. The book is a collection of scenes from Wiesel's personal experience, such as when he was separated from his mother and sisters at Auschwitz: "For a part of a second, I glimpsed my mother and my sisters moving

away to the right. Tzipora held Mother's hand. I saw them disappear into the distance; my mother was stroking my sister's fair hair . . . and I did not know that in that place, at that moment, I was parting from my mother and Tzipora forever."

Elie Wiesel listens to President George W. Bush speak at a Darfur exhibit at the Holocaust Memorial Museum in Washington, D.C.

REMAINING VIGILANT AND WATCHFUL

Unfortunately, the need to remain vigilant against future genocides is unlikely to diminish. As long as one political group can obtain power by marginalizing and dehumanizing another, the conditions for genocide can be created. Despite the lessons learned by the world after World War II and the Holocaust, mass killings have taken place in Cambodia from 1975–1979 (about 1.7 million killed), Rwanda in 1994 (up to 1 million

Images of Darfur, Sudan, and Chad are seen projected on the exterior walls of the Holocaust Memorial Museum in Washington, D.C., on November 20, 2006. The museum declared the crisis in Darfur a genocide emergency in 2004.

killed), and now Darfur (an estimated 200,000–450,000 people dead of disease or killed in violence as of late 2007). So, the fight continues even today, with Holocaust survivors and their descendants active in the effort to call attention to and halt genocidal killing wherever it may take place.

The U.S. Holocaust Memorial Museum's Committee on Conscience has played an active role in alerting the public to possible genocides or genocides in progress, such as in Darfur. Formed as a living memorial to the Holocaust, the group's mandate is to "alert the national conscience, influence policy makers, and stimulate worldwide action to confront and work to halt acts of genocide or related crimes against humanity." Groups like the Committee on Conscience are active around the world, and the memory of the Holocaust fuels their fight.

TIMELINE

1889 Adolf Hitler, the future leader of National Socialist (Nazi) Germany, is born.

1918 Germany capitulates to the Allies, ending World War I.

1925 *Mein Kampf*, Hitler's autobiography, is published.

1933 Laws are passed to ban Jews from practicing medicine or law, attending universities, belonging to the Journalists' Association, joining the civil service, or owning a farm.

1935 Hitler introduces the Nuremberg Laws, which strip German Jews of their citizenship and deprive them of civil rights.

1939 Germany occupies Poland, putting about two million more Jews under Nazi control.

1914 Germany enters World War I.

1923 The Nazi Party's Beer Hall Putsch, an attempt to seize power in Germany, fails, but Hitler receives a light sentence in a comfortable prison.

1933 The Nazi Party comes to power in Germany.

1933 Dachau, one of the first concentration camps, is opened in Germany.

1938 Kristallnacht, a national anti-Jewish riot, destroys thousands of businesses and places of worship. This is seen by many scholars as the start of the Holocaust.

1940 The Warsaw ghetto is established as a holding place for Jews; many die from disease and starvation there.

1941 More than 33,000 Jews are killed by Germans and Ukrainian police in the Babi Yar massacre outside of Kiev, Ukraine.

1942 The Wannsee Conference in Berlin is convened, and the decision is made to concentrate all of Europe's Jews into labor camps, with the intention of killing some or all of them in the process.

1942 The Warsaw ghetto is partially emptied, and 300,000 people are shipped by freight train to the Treblinka extermination camp.

1944 Jewish Sonderkommandos at Auschwitz stage an uprising; 250 Jews escape, but all are eventually recaptured and killed.

1941 During the Iasi pogrom in Romania, police and Romanian citizens kill as many as 14,000 Jews.

1941 The first fatal gassings of concentration camp prisoners take place in Auschwitz.

1942 Six major concentration camps are fully operational in Poland.

1943 Ghetto uprisings (including the Warsaw ghetto uprising) try and fail to prevent mass deportations through armed resistance.

1944 Germany occupies Hungary, putting another 800,000 Jews under Nazi control; more than half are shipped to Auschwitz, where most die.

1945 At the beginning of the year, death marches (where Jewish prisoners were marched to avoid the advance of the Soviet army) reach a peak. During one march, 60,000 prisoners were marched out of Auschwitz and 15,000 died.

1945 All remaining concentration camps are liberated by Allied forces.

1945 The war ends with Germany's total defeat by the Allies.

1945 Nuremberg Trials of German war criminals begin.

1948 The Jewish state of Israel is founded.

1993 The U.S. Holocaust Memorial Museum is dedicated and opened in Washington, D.C.

2004 The U.S. Holocaust Memorial Museum and the American Jewish World Service initiate the Save Darfur Coalition, a group of 150 faith-based advocacy and humanitarian aid groups dedicated to halting the genocide in Darfur, Sudan.

2007 The Jewish Council for Public Affairs places the Darfur genocide crisis at the top of its political agenda, officially making the issue a top priority for the Jewish community at the national and local level.

GLOSSARY

Allies In World War II, the major Allied powers included Britain, France, the Soviet Union, and the United States. They fought the Axis powers.

Axis In World War II, the major Axis powers included Germany, Italy, and Japan. They fought the Allied powers.

concentration camp Originally intended to hold enemies of the state and prisoners of war, concentration camps became a key part of Hitler's plan to destroy the Jews of Europe. Camps were generally some combination of prison, slave labor camp, extermination camp, and crematory (where bodies were burned). The largest and most notorious of the camps was Auschwitz, in Poland, where somewhere between one and five million people (mostly Jews) died.

dehumanize To make an enemy seem subhuman, animalistic, or pest-like, and therefore worthy of extermination. Before killing the Jews, the Nazis engaged in a long campaign to dehumanize them, comparing them to viruses or vermin (like rats or cockroaches). When Germans no longer regarded Jews as human beings, the idea of shipping former friends and neighbors away—never to return—became far easier to accept.

Einsatzgruppen While concentration camps were Hitler's preferred method for killing Jews in the west (such as the Jews of France, Germany, or western Poland), mobile groups of gunmen under the command of the SS called Einsatzgruppen were how many Jews were killed in the east (Russia, the Baltic States, Ukraine). An estimated one million (or more) Jews were killed in open-air shootings by these groups.

Final Solution Hitler's "Final Solution" referred to a plan for what he called the "Jewish problem," and it referred to the complete extermination of all of Europe's Jews.

genocide The deliberate destruction of an ethnic, religious, and/or national group. The Holocaust is the best-known modern genocide, but the Armenian, Cambodian, and Rwandan genocides are also major tragedies of the twentieth century. As of this writing, genocide is occurring in the Darfur region of Sudan.

Gestapo Hitler's feared secret police were known as the Gestapo, a contraction of the German words for "secret state police." The Gestapo was used to imprison and execute anyone seen as an enemy of the state, including student leaders, Jews, politically active Catholics, and Communists.

Israel In 1948, following World War II and the conclusion of the Holocaust, refugees founded a Jewish state in the Middle East. Israel was seen as a safe refuge for Jews and a guarantee that another Holocaust could never take place. It was also the realization of a longstanding dream known as Zionism, which called for a Jewish homeland in the biblical land of Israel.

Kristallnacht Also known as the Night of Broken Glass. On November 9 and 10, 1938, German authorities instigated an anti-Jewish riot largely directed at Jewish businesses. Many of these businesses had expensive, crystal glass windows that were shattered during the rioting. More than 7,000 Jewish businesses and over 1,500 synagogues were damaged or destroyed. In addition, Jews were physically assaulted, and cemeteries were desecrated.

Mein Kampf In English, "My Struggle." Hitler's autobiography, which warned of many of his future plans for Germany, including military expansion, and his hatred of Jews.

Nuremberg Laws A series of laws introduced by Hitler in 1935 that deprived Jews of their citizenship and civil rights, leaving them vulnerable to violence and imprisonment in concentration camps.

Nuremberg Trials After the conclusion of World War II, the Allied powers were left with the question of how to deal with German military and political leaders accused of war crimes and crimes against humanity. The trials were held from 1945 to 1949 in Nuremberg, Germany. The United States, the Soviet Union, and Great Britain were key in creating and overseeing the trials. Roughly two hundred Germans were tried for war crimes in the trials.

pogrom A riot directed against members of a specific group, typically an ethnic or religious minority. European Jews suffered pogroms at least as far back as the Crusades in the eleventh century. There were Muslim pogroms against Jews as well. These episodes of communal violence foreshadowed the Holocaust but were far smaller in scale and far less organized.

propaganda Information designed to help one political party gain and retain power. The information is not necessarily true or false, but it is always one-sided and designed to serve the party that creates it. Adolph Hitler was a master of propaganda, and anti-Jewish propaganda helped ordinary Germans accept (or turn a blind eye toward) the Holocaust.

Shoah A Hebrew word that literally means "calamity." Among many Jews, it is the preferred way to refer to what is commonly called the Holocaust.

Sonderkommandos Jewish work units forced to assist in the killings at the concentration camps.

Soviet Union A collection of states headed by what is now Russia, but including the Ukraine, Balkan republics, and numerous central Asian states. The Soviet Union was unified by the Communist Party, which maintained a lock on its government until its disintegration in 1991.

SS Two letters that stand for *Schutzstaffel*, which is German for "protective squadron." The SS was one of Nazi Germany's most feared military organizations. SS men staffed the concentration camps, serving as guards and administrators.

synagogue A Jewish place of worship. Many of Europe's synagogues were destroyed deliberately by Nazi Germany before and during World War II. They were specifically targeted during Kristallnacht in 1938.

Yad Vashem Israel's official museum dedicated to preserving the memory of those who perished in (or survived) the Holocaust.

FOR MORE INFORMATION

Anti-Defamation League
823 United Nations Plaza
New York, NY 10017
(212) 885-7700
Web site: http://www.adl.org

> The Anti-Defamation League aims to stop, by appeals to reason and conscience and, if necessary, by appeals to law, the defamation of the Jewish people. Its ultimate purpose is to secure justice and fair treatment to all citizens alike, and to put an end forever to unjust and unfair discrimination against and ridicule of any sect or body of citizens.

Holocaust Education Foundation
64 Old Orchard Road
Professional Building, Suite 520
Skokie, IL 60077
(847) 676-3700
Web site: http://www.holocaustef.org

> The Holocaust Educational Foundation is a private, nonprofit organization established in 1980 by survivors, their children, and their friends in order to preserve and promote awareness of the reality of the Holocaust.

Holocaust Teacher Resource Center
P.O. Box 6153
Newport News, VA 23606-6153
Web site: http://www.holocaust-trc.org

> The Holocaust Teacher Resource Center is dedicated to the memory of the six million Jewish people slaughtered during the Holocaust

and the millions other people slaughtered during the Nazi era. It strives to combat prejudice and bigotry by transforming the horrors of the Holocaust into positive lessons to help make this a better and safer world for everybody.

The Jewish Foundation for the Righteous
305 Seventh Avenue, 19th Floor
New York, NY 10001-6008
(212) 727-9955
Web site: http://www.jfr.org

The Jewish Foundation for the Righteous was established to fulfill the traditional Jewish commitment to *hakarat hatov*, the searching out and recognition of goodness. It provides financial assistance to aged and needy non-Jews who risked their lives to save Jews during the Holocaust. It also educates teachers and students about the history of the Holocaust.

USC Shoah Foundation Institute
P.O. Box 3168
Los Angeles, CA 90078-3168
(818) 777-7802
Web site: http://www.vhf.org

The USC Shoah Foundation Institute for Visual History and Education, with an archive of nearly 52,000 videotaped testimonies from Holocaust survivors and other witnesses, is part of the College of Letters, Arts & Sciences at the University of Southern California. The USC Shoah Foundation Institute works with a global network of partners to provide an array of valuable educational services that reach educators, students, and the general public around the world.

U.S. Holocaust Memorial Museum
100 Raoul Wallenberg Place SW

Washington, DC 20024-2126
(202) 488-0400
Web site: http://www.ushmm.org
In addition to its leadership training programs, the museum sponsors
onsite and traveling exhibitions, educational outreach, a Web site,
campus outreach, and Holocaust commemorations, including the
nation's annual observance in the U.S. Capitol. The museum's Center
for Advanced Holocaust Studies works to ensure the continued
growth and vitality of the field of Holocaust studies. As a living
memorial to the Holocaust, it works to prevent genocide in the
future through the Academy for Genocide Prevention, which trains
foreign policy professionals.

WEB SITES

Due to the changing nature of Internet links, Rosen Publishing has
developed an online list of Web sites related to the subject of this book.
This site is updated regularly. Please use this link to access the list:

http://www.rosenlinks.com/gmt/holoc

FOR FURTHER READING

Bauer, Yehuda. *A History of the Holocaust.* New York, NY: Franklin
Watts, 2002.

Des Chenes, Elizabeth, ed. *Genocide* (Contemporary Issues Companion).
Farmington Hills, MI: Greenhaven, 2007.

Frank, Anne. *The Diary of Anne Frank: The Revised Critical Edition.*
New York, NY: Doubleday, 2003.

Levi, Primo. *The Periodic Table.* New York, NY: Schocken, 1995.

Levi, Primo. *Surviving Auschwitz.* New York, NY: Barnes & Noble, 2007.

Oertelt, Henry A. *An Unbroken Chain: My Journey Through the Nazi
Holocaust.* Minneapolis, MN: Lerner Publications, 2000.

Opdyke, Irene. *In My Hands: Memories of a Holocaust Rescuer.* New York,
NY: Laurel Leaf, 2004.

Spiegelman, Art. *The Complete Maus.* New York, NY: Penguin Books, 2003.

Springer, Jane. *Genocide* (Groundwork Guides). Toronto, ON:
Groundwood Books, 2007.

Wiesel, Elie. *After the Darkness: Reflections of the Holocaust.* New York, NY:
Schocken, 2002.

Wiesel, Elie. *Dawn.* New York, NY: Hill & Wang, 2006.

Wiesel, Elie. *Day.* New York, NY: Hill & Wang, 2006.

Wiesel, Elie. *Night.* New York, NY: Hill & Wang, 2006.

Zullo, Allan, and Mara Bovsun. *Survivors: True Stories of Children in the
Holocaust.* New York, NY: Scholastic, 2005.

BIBLIOGRAPHY

Bauer, Yehuda. *Rethinking the Holocaust.* New Haven, CT: Yale University Press, 2001.

Berenbaum, Michael. *The World Must Know.* Washington, DC: United States Holocaust Museum, 2006.

Crowe, David M. *Oskar Schindler: The Untold Account of His Life, Wartime Activities, and the True Story Behind the List.* Philadelphia, PA: Westview Press, 2004.

Dwork, Deborah, and Robert Jan van Pelt. *Holocaust: A History.* New York, NY: W.W. Norton and Co., 2002.

Goldhagen, Daniel Jonah. *Hitler's Willing Executioners: Ordinary Germans and the Holocaust.* New York, NY: Alfred A. Knopf, 1996.

Greene, Joshua M., and Shiva Kumar. *Witness: Voices from the Holocaust.* New York, NY: The Free Press, 2000.

Iranek-Osmecki, Kazimierz. *He Who Saves One Life: The Complete, Documented Story of the Poles Who Struggled to Save Jews During World War Two.* New York, NY: Crown, 1971.

Kershaw, Ian. *Hitler: 1889–1936 Hubris.* New York, NY: W.W. Norton and Co., 1999.

Kershaw, Ian. *Hitler: 1936–1945 Nemesis.* New York, NY: W.W. Norton and Co., 2000.

Pringle, Heather. *The Master Plan: Himmler's Scholars and the Holocaust.* New York, NY: Hyperion, 2006.

Segev, Tom. *The Seventh Million: The Israelis and the Holocaust.* New York, NY: Henry Holt and Co., 1991.

Silver, Eric. "Is This the Real Schindler's List?" *Independent,* October 17, 1999.

INDEX

A

Allied forces, 6, 9, 30–31, 38, 39, 43, 44
Anielewicz, Mordechaj, 37
Auschwitz camp, 34, 37, 39–40, 42, 41, 44, 48
Austria, 8, 24, 43

B

Birkenau camp, 34, 37, 39

C

concentration camps, 6, 24, 27, 28, 29, 32, 34, 38–39
    liberation of, 39–40, 41
    survivors of, 43

D

death camps, 29, 33–36, 47
    treatment of people in, 34–36
    uprisings in, 36–37
death marches, 40–42
displaced persons, 43

E

Eichmann, Adolf, 33
Einsatzgruppen, 32, 33

F

"Final Solution," 30
Frank, Anne, 6, 27, 44
Frank, Hans, 31, 44, 47

G

gas chambers, 34, 36, 37, 44

genocide
    definition of, 4
    efforts to end, 48–49
    recent occurrences of, 48–49
German Workers' Party, 9
Gestapo, 13
ghettos, 28, 37, 47
Goebbels, Joseph, 18
Great Britain, 6, 9, 43
Gypsies/Roma, 20, 29, 37

H

Heydrich, Reinhard, 13, 33
Himmler, Heinrich, 32, 33
Hitler, Adolf, 4, 6, 7, 18, 28, 47
    beliefs/plans of, 12–13, 15, 24
    as chancellor of Germany, 15, 24
    declares boycott of Jewish businesses, 17
    personality of, 9–10, 11
    in prison/on trial, 11–13
    rise to power of, 9–12, 13–15, 20
    youth of, 8
Holocaust
    denial of, 41, 44
    evidence of, 44, 47
    Kristallnacht as beginning of, 26
    lesson to be learned from, 47, 48–49
    museums/memorials for, 45–47
    number of people killed, 4, 7, 18, 33
    people killed during, 6, 20, 37–38
    resistance during, 7, 21, 36–37
    role of ordinary Germans in, 20–23

Holocaust Remembrance Day, 47

I

Israel, 43, 47
Italy, 10, 41, 43

J

Jews
after WWII, 43
boycott against businesses of, 17–19
during WWI, 8, 27
in Germany before WWII, 6–7, 16
prejudice against, 6, 8, 16, 17, 18, 19,
21–24, 26–28, 43
killing of during Holocaust, 4, 6, 7,
13, 18, 31–32, 33–34, 37–38

K

Kristallnacht, 18, 26, 28

L

Levi, Primo, 41, 44

M

Mein Kampf, 12–13

N

Nazi Party/Nazi Germany
beliefs of, 12–13
killing of Jews, 7, 31–32, 33–34
plan for "master race," 19–20, 24, 32
prejudice against Jews, 6, 8, 16, 17, 19,
21–24, 26–28
restrictions/laws imposed by, 15, 19, 26
rise of, 6, 9–11, 13–15, 16, 18, 27
Netherlands, 7, 27, 38

Nuremberg Rally, 24
Nuremburg Trials, 31, 32, 44–45, 47

P

Poland, 7, 28, 32, 33–34, 37, 38, 47

Q

Quisling, Vidkun, 38

S

Schindler, Oskar, 21
Simon Wiesenthal Center, 46
slave labor, 29, 30
Sonderkommandos, 37
Soviet Union, 4, 6 , 39, 41
prisoners of war from, 29–30
SS, 28, 32, 33, 36, 37, 38
sterilizations, forced, 12, 19

T

Treaty of Versailles, 9, 12, 15
Treblinka camp, 33–34, 36

U

United States, 6, 39, 43
U.S. Holocaust Memorial Museum, 34,
45–47
Committee on Conscience, 49

W

Wannsee Conference 13, 30–32, 33
Wiesel, Elie, 44, 48
World War I, Germany and, 8, 9, 27
World War II, 4, 6, 29–31, 38, 48
end of, 7, 39–42

Y

Yad Vashem Memorial, 45

ABOUT THE AUTHOR

James Norton is a writer based in Minneapolis, Minnesota. He holds a degree in history from the University of Wisconsin-Madison and has worked as an international news editor, political journalist, and food writer. He is the founder and editor of *Flak Magazine*.

PHOTO CREDITS